First published 2025
This edition © Wooden Books Ltd 2025

Published by Wooden Books Ltd.
Glastonbury, Somerset.
www.woodenbooks.com

British Library Cataloguing in Publication Data
Davis, K.W.
Hermeticism

A CIP catalogue record for this book
may be obtained from the British Library.

ISBN-10: 1-907155-53-8
ISBN-13: 978-1-907155-53-6

All rights reserved.
For permission to reproduce any part of this
jewel of a book please contact the publishers.

Designed and typeset in Glastonbury, UK.
Printed in India on FSC® certified papers by
Quarterfold Printabilities Pvt. Ltd.

The Ouroboros
End and Beginning

LEFT: A human, seeing a distant star, collapses the wavefunction of the photon of light. This photon has travelled across space, but not across time, as photons, travelling at the speed of light, do not experience time. Thus, according to John Wheeler, "We are participators in bringing into being not only the near and here but the far away and long ago".

BELOW: The large scale structure of the universe is one of nodes connected by electrical plasma filaments, much like the structure of the human brain. Could the cosmos really be a vast mind, as the Hermeticists always said?

FACING PAGE: Convergent evolution perfects the same solutions again and again, from different starting points. Reptiles, fish, and mammals have all perfected the same ideal form for swimming fast. The same solutions are found in flying animals, marsupials, and placentals too. Striving towards perfect forms is a deeply Hermetic idea.

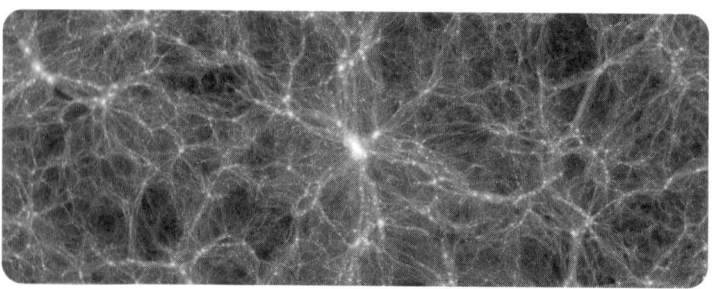

THE CONSCIOUS UNIVERSE
the art of self-perfection

In the 1970s cosmologists noticed a problem. The more they perfected the Standard Models of physics and cosmology, the more it seemed as though the universe had been born optimised for life. Fiddle with any of nature's constants, even slightly (e.g. the strength of gravity relative to the strength of the electromagnetic force, or the mass of the proton relative to the mass of the neutron), and no life could exist.

Some theologians claimed that science had proven the existence of a Divine creator. Some scientists claimed there was an infinite multiverse of universes, each with their own constants, most stillborn except for rare jewels like our own (the Hermeticist Giordano Bruno was murdered for a similar suggestion in 1600). Physicist John Wheeler argued that the universe could have been perfected by conscious observers like us, raising humans to an important role in the scheme of things once more, another Hermetic idea (*opposite top*). Others have pointed to an electric universe, with stars and galaxies connected by plasma filaments in a structure resembling a vast brain (*lower opposite*)— a conscious universe, yet another Hermetic idea. Like convergent evolution (*below*) and the Great Work of alchemy, the universe is polished into a perfect form.

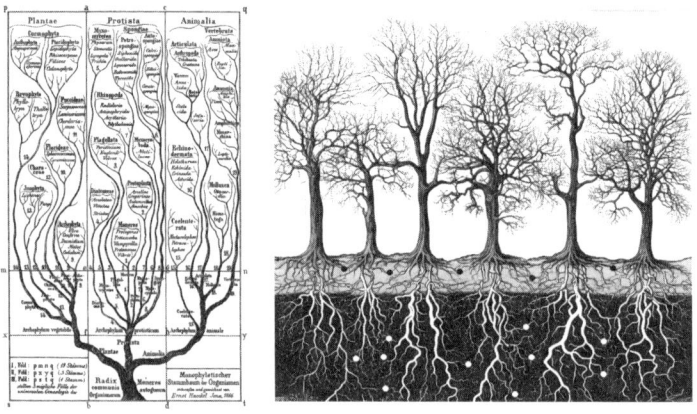

ABOVE: Entanglement, whether genetic, chemical, physical, ecological, informational, social, economic, or personal, is a Hermetic perception now generalised in the sciences.

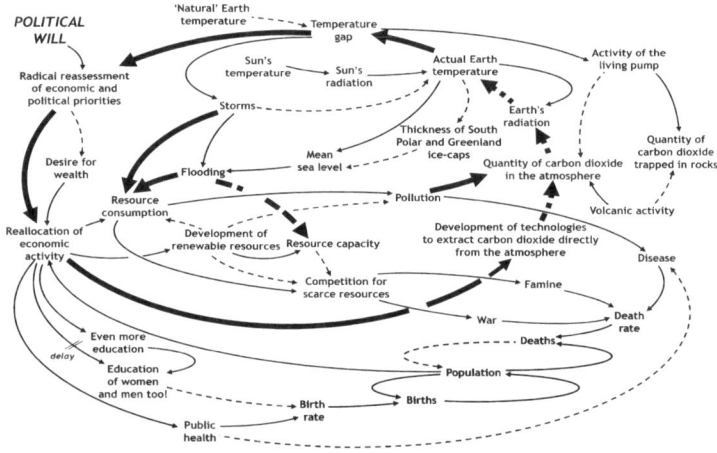

ABOVE: A modern systems diagram incorporating feedback loops from Earth systems science and sociology, demonstrating the Hermetic axiom "Everything is Connected". Dennis Sherwood.

Everything is Connected
complexity and systems

Hermetic ideas continued to resurface throughout the 20th century. The idea that *"everything is light"* found its modern parallel in Einstein's famous equation $E=mc^2$, which relates energy, mass and the speed of light (*below*). Another Hermetic precept that has also come back into fashion is that *"everything is interconnected with everything else through a mesh of interlocking relationships"* (*page 34*). Newton and Einstein had already shown how every object in the universe influences every other via gravitation, and in the 20th century it was also found that two nearby particles can be quantum entangled so that they affect one another even when moved light-years apart, leading some to suggest that the entire universe might be superconnected. And it was soon connected in other ways too, as by the 21st century, most social, economic, chemical, biological, and Earth-system scientists were also talking about their subjects in terms of complex interconnected systems (*opposite bottom*).

Even the alchemical vision came of age. The elements of the everyday physical world turned out to be just four fundamental particles interacting via just four forces. Just six elements (hydrogen, oxygen, carbon, nitrogen, sulphur, and phosphorus) make up most of all living things. And modern chemical processes still involve the separation, refinement, and recombination of elements to build the materials so useful to us today. Just like the alchemists were doing, all those centuries ago.

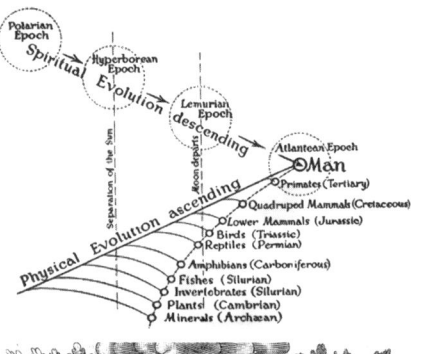

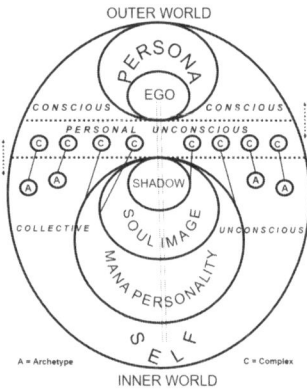

TOP LEFT: Rudolph Steiner's diagram of the convergence of spiritual and physical evolution in humankind. ABOVE: Carl Jung's model of the human psyche. LEFT: Jakob Böhme's diagram of God as a binary, recursive being. To know Himself, God first divides into positive and negative aspects. BELOW: Our illusory three-dimensional space is defined by the two boundaries of opacity (Satan) and material condensation (Adam). William Blake, Milton, c.1806.

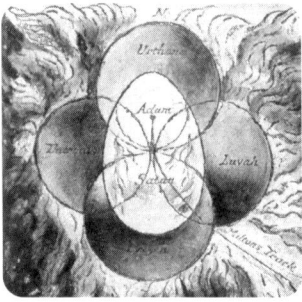

The Perennial Tradition
continuity through the centuries

Hermeticists continually reappear through history. The mystic Jakob Böhme [1575–1624], influenced by Paracelcus' writings on the micro-macrocosm and the transformative power of alchemy, held that *"all that is is light"*—a direct inheritance from the *Poimandres*. The Swedish mystic Emanuel Swedenborg [1688-1772], influenced by Böhme and other Hermetic, Gnostic and Neoplatonic sources, held that the inner eye can see the spiritual cause behind the natural effect.

William Blake [1757–1827] drew from both the 'optimistic' Hermetic stream of thinking (that matter is created by the Divine and is therefore good) and the more 'pessimistic' Gnostic threads (that human souls have fallen into 'evil' matter). Like Böhme he thought that the inward eye sees the principle or quality, and the outward sees the physical form. His marriage of microcosm and macrocosm (*"to see the world in a grain of sand"*) also reveals Hermetic influence.

Polymath Johann Wolfgang von Goethe [1749–1832] modelled his tragi-comic magus Dr. Faustus on the Hermetic alchemical magicians of the past. His archetypal plant (a synthesis of the transformative imagination of nature that can only be apprehended by our own transformative imaginative faculty) echoes the *'like is known by like'* or *'Nous* is needed to understand *the Nous'* in the *Poimandres* dialogue.

Other notable Hermeticists include the English poet Samuel Taylor Coleridge [1772–1834], French esotericist Eliphas Lévi [1810–1875], Austrian architect Rudolf Steiner [1861–1925], Swiss psychologist Carl Jung [1875–1961], French Egyptologist R. A. Schwaller de Lubicz [1887–1961], and Czech occultist Franz Bardon [1909–1958].

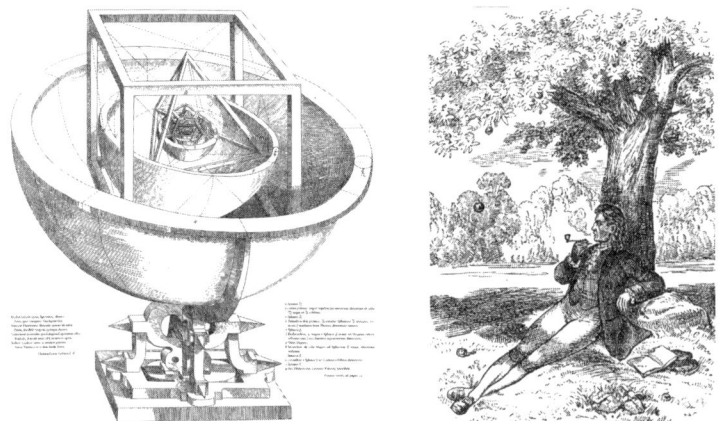

ABOVE: LEFT: Kepler's model of the orbits of the six known heliocentric planets spaced by the five Platonic solids. This was an early attempt to marry two idealised systems, the goal of the sciences.
RIGHT: Isaac Newton deduces the existence of gravity from a falling apple. Newton spent decades studying Hermetic and alchemical texts, as he sought to penetrate the mysteries of Nature.

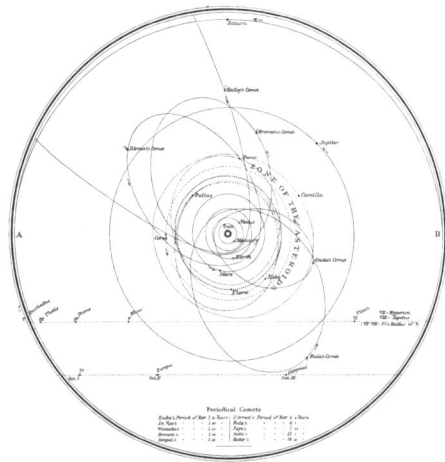

LEFT: Early plot of the elliptical paths of comets in the solar system. Kepler's and Newton's Laws (and those that followed) made society aware that the physical world around us is governed by abstract mathematical laws. From the buildings we live in to the devices we use in them, the modern world today relies on these theorems and the Hermetic assumption which ties them to the physical world. And just like the strange formulations of the alchemists, mathematical and physical equations are only intelligible to trained initiates.

THE AGE OF LAWS
mathematical models of nature

Over 2,500 years ago, the Greek philosopher Pythagoras [c.570–495 BC] recognised that simple fractions produce pleasant musical harmonies (*below*). Then Archimedes [c.287–211 BC] noticed that an object always displaces its own weight when put in a liquid. Some 2,000 years later Johannes Kepler [1571–1630] wrote down his three laws of planetary motion, on which Isaac Newton [1643–1727] based his law of universal gravitation and three laws of motion.

The Hermetic principles *"As above, so below"* and *"Follow Nature"* are the cornerstones of modern scientific thought. Even the early Greek examples above illustrate how science is an edifice built on theorems, and theorems are models built on the fundamental assumption that a realm of abstract mathematical laws ('above') govern the workings of the material world ('below'). As Galileo Galilei famously wrote in 1623, ten years before he was arrested:

> *"The book of nature was written not in words and letters, but with characters, mathematics, geometric figures, and numbers".*

 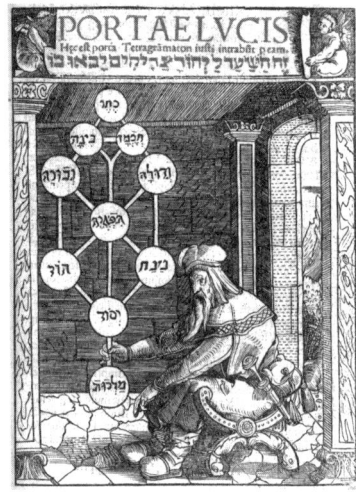

ABOVE: Left: Stonemasons at work. The practical operations of stonemasonry were symbolized in Freemasonry as tools to improve the initiate's character. RIGHT: The Hermetic Order of the Golden Dawn, London 1888, had a complex grade system based on the Kabbalistic Tree of Life.

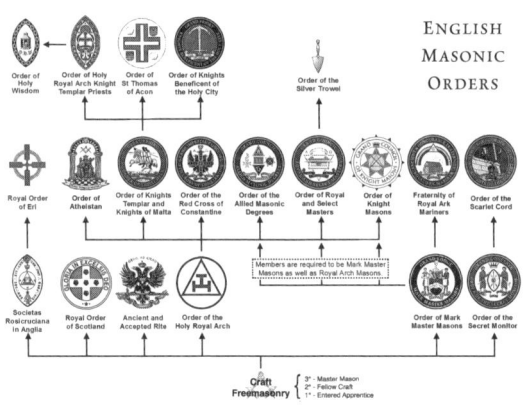

ENGLISH MASONIC ORDERS

LEFT: Some of the many modern Masonic degrees and orders in England and Wales. The York Rite has further degrees, as does the Ancient Accepted Scottish Rite (up to the 33rd degree), plus there are Social Group and Women's Orders. Other countries have yet further orders. To find out more you will need to join!

SECRET ORDERS
freemasons and occultists

During the Middle Ages, the crafts (stonemasons, goldsmiths, and others) organized into guilds and met in buildings called 'lodges'. During the Renaissance, many also developed an interest in the liberal arts, sciences, and esotericism (influenced by Hermeticism). In 1717 a Grand Lodge of Freemasonry was founded in London to teach these to initiates, free of the original craft. By the mid Enlightenment, Freemasonry's emphasis on the right to one's own political and religious beliefs would influence many of the Masons who went on to found the United States of America in the 1770s to 1780s.

Masonic initiates today receive instruction in the arts and sciences, and in personal growth and morality. They are initiated with symbol and ceremony into 'degrees', usually three; meetings are restricted to members. Their secret handshakes and passwords derive from the signs used by medieval masons to identify their level of expertise.

Other orders have come and gone. A popular example, the Hermetic Order of the Golden Dawn was founded in 1888. An occult school, inti ally popular amongst intellectuals and artists, it began with good intentions but soon fell into decadence with many of the Victorian occultists spending more time throwing curses at each other than living according to the precepts of Hermeticism, despite their regalia, ceremony and fine words.

ABOVE: The well-defended and mobile 'Collegium Fraternitatis' (College of the Brotherhood) from Speculum Sophicum Rhodo-Stavroticum (The Philosophical Mirror of the Rosy Cross) by Daniel Mögling [1596-1635] under the pseudonym Teophilus Schweighardt Constantiens.

THE CROSS & THE ROSE
the chymical wedding

Between 1610 and 1616, three 'manifestos' were published in Germany, recounting events in the life of one C.R.C. (later identified as Christian Rosenkreutz). According to the first two manifestos—the *Fama Fraternitatis* (Fame of the Brotherhood) and the *Confessio Fraternitatis* (Confession of the Brotherhood)—C.R.C. was born in Germany in 1378 and accompanied his spiritual master on a wisdom-seeking tour of the Middle East. The master died along the way, and C.R.C. continued the journey on his own, finding exoteric and esoteric teachers along his route. He returned home by way of Egypt, North Africa, and Spain, studying local wisdom as he travelled.

Back in Germany, C.R.C. established an order of eight men, all Doctors of Medicine and all virgins. They were required to live by six rules: (1) To heal the sick for free; (2) To wear the clothing of the country they are in; (3) To meet annually at a given place, the House of the Spirit, or write to explain their absence; (4) To each find a man to replace him after his death; (5) To use the word C.R. as a kind of password; and (6) To keep the brotherhood secret for a century.

The third manifesto, *The Chymical Wedding of Christian Rosenkreutz*, tells the story of C.R.C. attending a royal wedding in a miraculous castle in 1459. Packed with alchemical, astrological, and magical allegories, the extraordinary story unfolds over seven days.

We know now that the manifestos were all works of fiction, but at the time, scholars all over Europe (including a young Descartes) accepted the accounts, and sought strenuously to find the fraternity and gain admission.

ABOVE: The 11th key (of 12) by Basilus Valentinus. The elements are purified and separated.
BELOW: An alchemist's laboratory, showing the equipment and operations. P. Bruegel.

Solve et Coagula
fix the volatile and make volatile the fixed

The outer, laboratory work of alchemy (transforming substances) is mirrored by inner, spiritual work (self-transformation). Thus calcination (burning a substance to ashes) is a form of purification.

Take the alchemical saying *"The sum of our art is to make fixed what is volatile and make volatile what is fixed"*. In a laboratory, this will involve precipitating salts from solutions, and dissolving solids in solvents, but it also means disciplining the mind and emotions, and breaking down fixed ideas. The same theme appears in the maxim *Solve et Coagula* "*Separate and Recombine*". In a laboratory, an alchemist might purify a compound by refining it into its constituent elements and recombining them, but in a personal context this might mean separating emotions from the intellect before speaking, or remaining aware of the difference between spirit and soul, or breaking down complex ideas and putting them back together in a new way. Each way, they are perfecting their stone.

The Great Work proceeds via a series of stages. The first, the *Nigredo* (Blackening), is the stage of putrefaction of the *prima materia*, the "death" of the old form, the confrontation with the shadow and the dissolving of the ego, and is sometimes achieved via fermentation. The second stage, the *Albedo* (Whitening), involves purification (distillation and sublimation). The final stage is the *Rubedo* (Reddening), where spirit and matter are recombined in perfect balance, unifying the soul with the Divine to produce the miracle of the Philosopher's Stone.

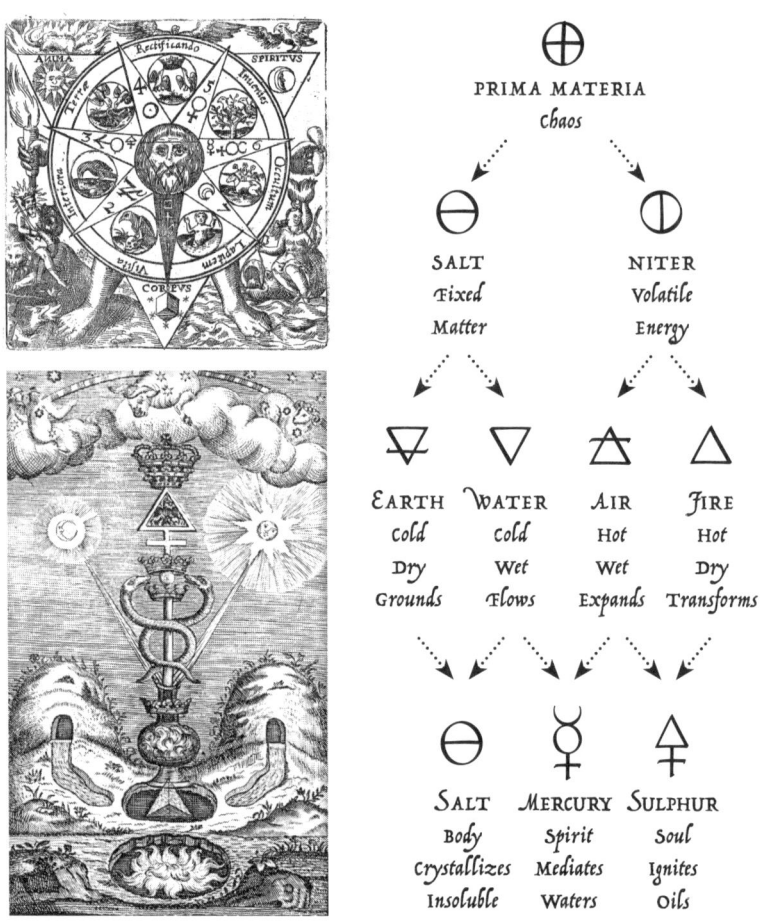

TOP LEFT: The Magnum Opus. The four elements appear in the four corners, the three principles in the tips of a triangle. Between the spokes of the seven planets are the seven words of the VITRIOL formula. ABOVE LEFT: Soul as the central axis around which reflection and realisation dance.

THE ALCHEMIST'S ART
matter as spirit and spirit as matter

Alchemy involves the transformation and perfection of substances (material, spiritual and philosophical) from lower base forms (e.g. lead) to higher refined forms (e.g. gold). Alongside the four elements (Fire, Earth, Air and Water) it uses the principles of SULPHUR (Soul), and MERCURY (Spirit), to understand the nature of things. Paracelsus later expanded these to the *tria prima* with the addition of SALT (Body). The *Magnum Opus* or 'Great Work' of alchemy is to produce the mysterious substance known as the Philosopher's Stone (often symbolised as a red lion) from the raw *Prima Materia* (*opposite right*).

Lesser works were also undertaken, such as producing pure oils from plants, which captured their soul, or paint pigments from rocks and metals, which might change colour when heated. Modern chemistry would later emerge from the careful experiments of the alchemists.

The alchemist Basilius Valentinus [1394–1450] famously recorded the VITRIOL motto: *Visita Interiora Terrae Rectificando Invenies Occultum Lapidem*, *"Visit the interior of the Earth and by rectification you will find the hidden stone"* (*opposite top left*). This suggests not only a mining and refining expedition, but also the process of personal purification central to alchemy. The stone is not only out there in the world, but is also our soul, our character. Alchemists seek to perfect both. They are the same thing.

Moon	Mercury	Venus	Sun	Mars	Jupiter	Saturn
Silver	Quicksilver	Copper	Gold	Iron	Tin	Lead
Reflection	Mediation	Harmony	Realisation	Force	Expansion	Limitation

LEFT: The Sigillum Dei, "Seal of God" of John Dee [1527–1608], magician of his age and astrologer to Queen Elizabeth I. It is labelled with the names of God and the angels. With his partner Edward Kelley, Dee restored the Enochian language of the angels. In the 1590s they travelled through northern Europe to the court of King Rudolf II in Prague, a city built by alchemists, and met key players in the northern Renaissance, such as Giordano Bruno, Tycho Brahe and Johannes Kepler. Many of the houses they visited would, only thirty years later, produce many of the great alchemical tomes of the period.

LEFT: Scene from The Tempest. Shakespeare modelled his famous archmage Prospero on John Dee, and incorporated many Hermetic and Platonic ideas into his work, including from alchemy and mythology. Many of his greatest lines have Hermetic roots: "to take upon ourselves the mystery of things as if we were God's spies" echoes the Eusebeia of the Hermeticists. Ted Hughes argues that Shakespeare developed his core mythology to bridge the rift between Catholics and Puritans.

MEDIATION
between the worlds

Hermetic mediation involves communication and influence between different planes of existence via intermediary beings and forces: planetary intelligences, angels and daimons, elemental beings, natural forces and powers, and sacred names, words, letters, and numbers.

Each planet has a spirit or intelligence that mediates its influences on Earth. For example, the spirit of Venus mediates forces of harmony and beauty, while Saturn's intelligence channels forces of limitation and structure. A Hermeticist working with these might time their operations according to planetary hours, or create talismans during specific astronomical configurations to better receive their influences.

Elemental beings (*salamanders* of fire, *sylphs* of air, *undines* of water, and *gnomes* of earth) also act as intermediaries. A practitioner working with plant medicines might invoke the help of elemental beings to better mediate the healing properties of herbs and minerals.

Angels and daimons also mediate between the divine and material realms, and can be invoked in ceremonial operations or consulted for knowledge of natural processes. Humans, standing at the intersection of the spiritual and material realms, can work consciously with these intelligences to raise lower matters to higher states of perfection, ensuring that divine influence reaches all levels of creation.

The calling or writing of divine names can also be useful for mediation (*see Kircher's international wheel opposite page 1*). The English occultist John Dee [1527–1608] claimed he could communicate with the angel Uriel and obtain material channelled in Enochian angel language during spiritual conferences with his colleague Edward Kelley (*see opposite*).

LEFT: A Christian Virtue Tree, made of seven clusters of circles with the names of the seven Virtues and their seven Subsidiaries. At the top, two angels stand next to 'Peace' and 'Piety' beside the head of Christ, atop Faith (V), Charity (VII), and Hope (VI). At the base of the tree, Humility, the root of the virtues, is represented by the Annunciation. On either side, the personifications of the virtues with their attributes; Prudence (I) with a dove; Justice (III) holds a palm branch and scales; Fortitude (II) a sword and shield; Temperance (IIII) a chalice and cornucopia of fire. Psalter of Robert de Lisle. c.1310.

BELOW: A table of virtues and vices based on Aristotle's Nichomachean ethics, in which virtues are the mean between extremes of excess and deficiency. The private chapel of the Medicis in Palazzo Medici Riccardi in Florence has a fourteen circle design on the floor, so you walk the virtuous balance, with seven excesses on your left, seven deficiencies on your right.

Other Hermetic scholars flourished at the same time: Nicolas Flamel [1330-1418], Pico della Mirandola [1463-1494], Agrippa [1486-1535], Paracelsus [1493-1541], Nostradamus [1503-1566], John Dee [1527-1608], Giordano Bruno [1548-1600], Isaac Casaubon [1559-1614] and Robert Fludd [1574-1637]. They all believed in correspondences between the microcosm and the macrocosm, seeing nature as a living, symbolic text to be "read". All sought the universal principles underlying nature and spirit, and the transformation of both.

DEFICIENCY	VIRTUE	EXCESS
TOO LITTLE	JUST RIGHT	TOO MUCH
Arrogance	Humility	Abasement
Carelessness	Prudence	Pusillanimity
Indulgence	Temperance	Abstinence
Stinginess	Generosity	Profligacy
Despair	Hope	Presumption
Cowardice	Courage	Foolhardiness
Corruption	Integrity	Legalism
Slothfulness	Diligence	Workaholism

THE RENAISSANCE
rebirth of the ancient dream

During the Middle Ages, Hermeticism withdrew from sight in Western Europe as all things 'magical' were censored. But the secret tradition lived on. In the thirteenth century the Dominican friar Thomas Aquinas [c.1225–1274] combined Hermetic theory with the teachings of Judaism and Christianity. Other Christian scholars soon equated the alchemical Philosopher's Stone with the Holy Grail and Jesus. Pope Alexander VI [1431-1503] placed Hermetic and astrological symbols on a fresco in the Vatican, and had the figure of Hermes Trismegistus placed on the marble floor of Siena Cathedral (*see page 9*).

From the 14th century, the Italian Renaissance brought a rebirth of Hermetic theory and practice to the West. Around 1460 the monk Leonardo da Pistoia [1502–1548] found a copy of the *Corpus Hermeticum* in Macedonia and presented it to Cosimo de' Medici in Florence. Cosimo took it to Marsilio Ficino, who was translating Plato into Latin, and asked him to translate the *Hermeticum* first. The resulting fusion of ancient Greek and Hermetic thought ignited a golden era of intense discovery, from the fifth element suggested by the five Platonic solids (*right*) to rediscovered systems of virtue ethics (*facing page*).

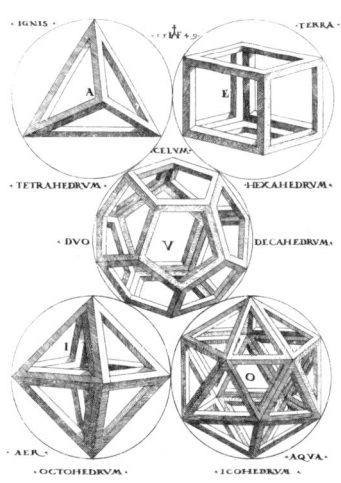

LEFT: Early church and cathedral builders were steeped in the Hermetic arts, from the use of number, geometry and harmonics that guided the design of their plans, elevations, windows and decorations, to the alchemical knowledge of metal oxides used to dye their stained glass (such as the famous cobalt blue glass at Chartres).

BELOW: The Seven Liberal Arts (Grammar, Logic, Rhetoric, Arithmetic, Geometry, Music and Astronomy) arranged as seven groups of people around the central character of Temperance, symbolizing balance. The studies of arithmetic, harmony, geometry, and logic would later inspire Newton and Kepler to discover the hidden rules of planetary motion.

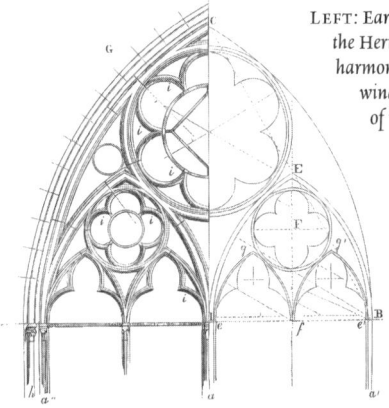

HERMETIC RELIGIONS
early Christian and Arabic Hermeticism

Hermetic influences are evident in early Christianity. The Gnostics had a similar creation scheme, except with a Demiurge (an evil usurper who stole the cosmos). The Manichaeans, once a world religion with millions of followers, saw Jesus as a figure of light, much like Hermetic *Nous*, and counted Hermes Trismegistus as one of their prophet Mani's forerunners. The Bogomils and the Cathars both held that Mary was sent by the *Nous* so Jesus could be born as its earthly incarnation. The Cathars' sacrament of *consolamentum* sought to cast out '*demons*' with the fire of the holy spirit, similar to Hermetic 'soul medicine'. Even the first Christian *hermit*, St. Paul the Anchorite, came from Thebes, home to the great Egyptian temples of Luxor and Karnac.

More Hermetic texts survive in Arabic than in any other language, and Hermes is cited in Arabic scientific literature from the eighth century. Jabir Al-Hayan [c.721–815 AD], father of 'algebra', wrote Hermetic texts that became very influential in European alchemy.

The cathedral builders used the Hermetic arts, such as geometry and harmony, in their work (*see opposite*). Chivalry also has Hermetic roots. In Wolfram Von Effenbach's epic story *Parsival*, a knight searches for the Holy Grail (an image of *Nous*, *right*).

PLANET	METAL	ORGAN	COLOUR	DAY	ANIMAL	STONE	TREE	HERB
MOON	Silver	Brain	White	Monday	Cat	Pearl	Birch	Jasmine
MERCURY	Mercury	Lungs	Orange	Wednesday	Fox	Opal	Hazel	Fennel
VENUS	Copper	Kidneys	Green	Friday	Dove	Emerald	Apple	Rose
SUN	Gold	Heart	Yellow	Sunday	Lion	Citrine	Ash	Chamomile
MARS	Iron	Gallbladder	Red	Tuesday	Wasp	Ruby	Holly	Ginger
JUPITER	Tin	Liver	Blue	Thursday	Eagle	Saphire	Oak	Sage
SATURN	Lead	Spleen	Black	Saturday	Snake	Obsidian	Yew	Comfrey

ABOVE: Table of typical correspondences. BELOW: Athanasius Kircher's astrological chart showing the various organs of the body, their planetary rulerships, and a table of medical conditions and appropriate herbs, 1646. FACING PAGE: Athanasius Kircher's Sunflowers, revealing the analogy of form and homonym (the planetary rulerships of plants may be found in their names).

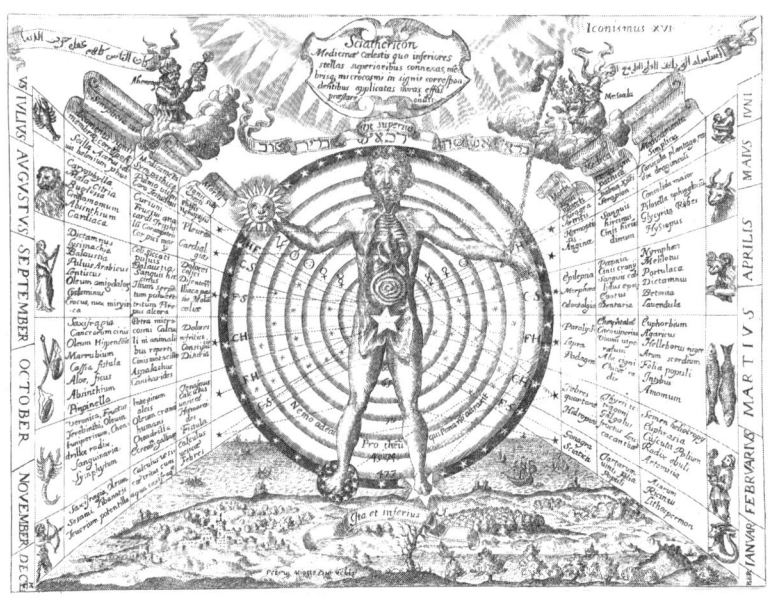

MAGIC & MEDICINE
signatures and talking statues

In Hermeticism, the qualities, forms, and flavours of things—minerals, plants, animals, landscape—reveal their interconnections to each other and to the seven governors above. Humans, universes in miniature, embody the same correspondences, which then influence each other through the principle of *sympathy*, known in later European tradition as *The Doctrine of Signatures*. Because Nature, inseminated by the *Logos*, mirrors the light world of *Nous*, all forms of nature recall forms of the divine mind. Magical arts concern themselves with understanding these forms, so their qualities can be harnessed in the realm of *Nous*.

Texts such as the *Cyranides* give formulas for talismans and preparations to bring success, healing, and protections, often balancing the four elements in their ingredients. The *Liber Sacer* deals with astrological botany, as does *From Hermes Trismegistus to Asclepius: On Plants and the Seven Planets* and *On the Plants of the Twelve Signs*.

Another text, *The Holy Book of Hermes to Asclepius*, deals with plants in relation to the decans (*see page 32*) as a basis for botanical prescriptions. *The Brontologion* uses the timing of thunder to make predictions while *The Peri Seismōn* uses earthquakes. Perhaps strangest of all is telestikē, the Græco-Egyptian art of ensouling statues, which is discussed in the *Asclepius*.

SECRETS OF THE STARS
the ancient art of astrology

The Hermetic principle '**As above, so below**' underpins the practice of astrology, where the positions and alignments of the heavenly bodies are held to correspond with events on Earth. A form of recognizable astrology arises in Mesopotamia in the 6th century CE, emerging as Hellenistic astrology in Egypt around the time the oldest known works of the Technical Hermetica were being compiled.

Astrology is crucial for selecting propitious timings in the alchemical process and in other magical arts, including medical diagnosis and treatment with astrologically aligned herbs and stones (*p.34*). Book XVI of the *Poimandres* discusses how a person's character is defined at the moment of their birth by the positions of the seven governors: the Sun, Moon, Mercury, Venus, Mars, Jupiter and Saturn (*below left*). These ruled specific 10° segments (decans) of the zodiac, and moved through the stages of the twelve zodiacal signs (*below right*). The natal arrangement reveals a person's passions, the *daimons* attached to them, and the tools to oppose them.

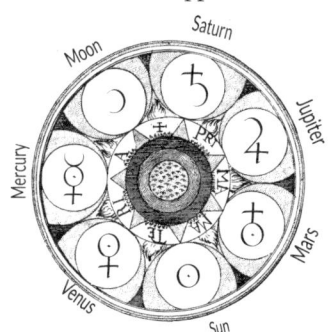

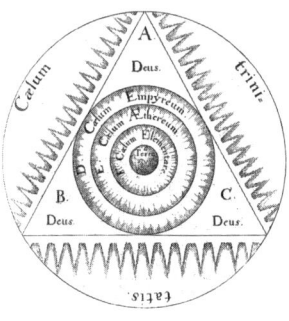

ABOVE: "You who imitate the work of Nature, must seek four spheres, within which a gentle fire moves. Let the first represent Vulcan, and the second show Mercury, while the third sphere holds the Moon. The fourth, Apollo, is yours, and the fire of Nature is perceived. Let that chain guide your hands in your art." From Atalanta Fugiens by Michael Maier, Frankfurt 1618.
LEFT: The trinitarian heaven surrounds the empyreal fiery heaven, the ethereal heaven, and the elemental heaven. FACING PAGE: In alchemical images the soul is often depicted as a treasure concealed within the Earth.

LIGHTS IN THE MIND
eusebeia, ekstasis, gnosis

The Hermetic texts encourage regular praise and love for the beauty of creation. To aid this, a heart-opening virtue named *Eusebia* (piety) is developed in preparation for the more rigorous transformation of the soul. *Eusebeia* is the attitude of wonder, admiration and awe, when faced with the Divine, and is cultivated in the same way as Plato's veneration of the Good, the True and the Beautiful.

A related Hermetic concept is the state of *Ekstasis* (ecstacy), literally 'standing outside oneself' or 'being displaced'. This can be induced by meditation, or inhaling the smoke from incense, or ingesting certain herbs and stones, sometimes in darkness, to assist the manifestation of the divine light, as described by Zosimos of Panopolis [c.260–340 CE] and the Syrian neoplatonic philosopher Iamblichus [c.245–325 CE].

Hermetic *Gnosis* is a different order of state again (*see page 24*). Gnosis can only be achieved by the hard work of the practitioner, to heal and enlighten their soul. This is a salvational state of knowledge, the embodiment of light, of *Nous* within the life of the soul. Hermetic Gnosis is initiatory, not in the symbolic ceremonial sense of Masonic or Rosicrucian orders (*see pages 46–49*), but is instead an initiation earned through conscious suffering and pursuit of the light of wisdom. It cannot be bought or bargained for, only bestowed by the Divine.

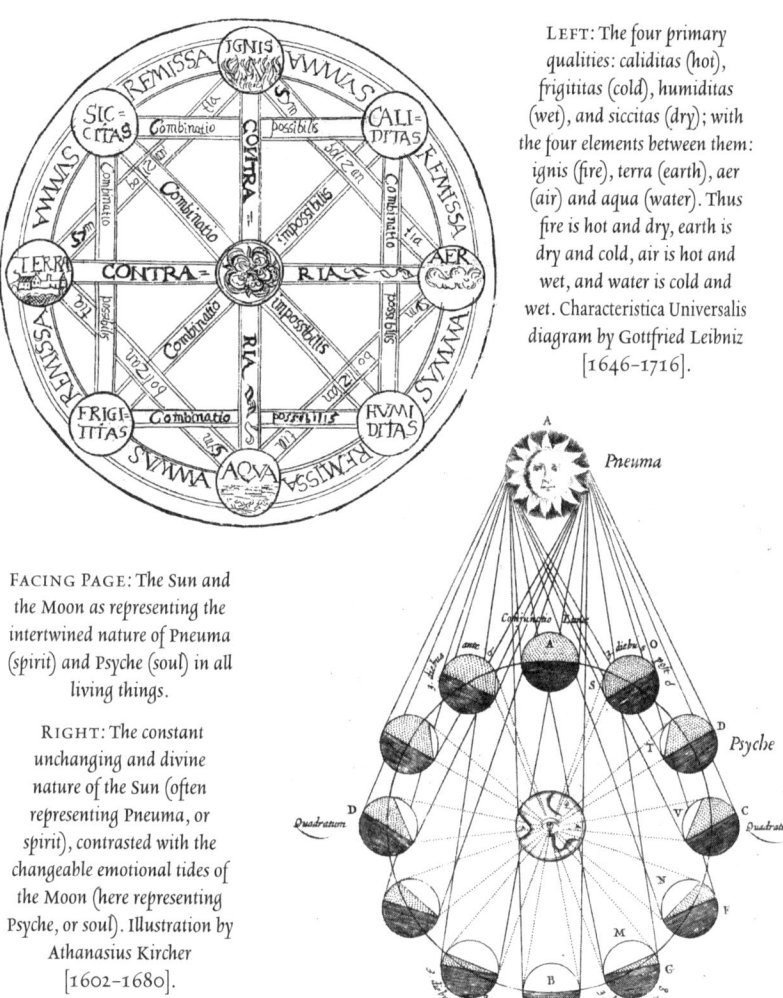

LEFT: The four primary qualities: caliditas (hot), frigititas (cold), humiditas (wet), and siccitas (dry); with the four elements between them: ignis (fire), terra (earth), aer (air) and aqua (water). Thus fire is hot and dry, earth is dry and cold, air is hot and wet, and water is cold and wet. Characteristica Universalis diagram by Gottfried Leibniz [1646-1716].

FACING PAGE: The Sun and the Moon as representing the intertwined nature of Pneuma (spirit) and Psyche (soul) in all living things.

RIGHT: The constant unchanging and divine nature of the Sun (often representing Pneuma, or spirit), contrasted with the changeable emotional tides of the Moon (here representing Psyche, or soul). Illustration by Athanasius Kircher [1602-1680].

Pneuma & Psyche
spirit and soul

In Hermetic philosophy, spirit (*pneuma*) and soul (*psyche*) are distinct but related principles, and telling them apart is one of the core tasks.

Spirit is the divine principle, associated with pure consciousness or divine intelligence (*Nous*). Connected to the hot elements of fire and air, it can be imagined as a direct emanation of divine mind. Spirit is the universal animating principle that gives life, the mediator between divine and human realms. It is often associated with the higher mental faculties. Your pneuma is that part of you which is truly divine.

Soul is the intermediate principle between spirit and body. It is more individual and personal than spirit. Connected to the cold elements of water and earth, soul is the seat of emotions, desires, and individual consciousness. More closely tied to the material world than spirit, it is the principle that gives form to matter, and animates the vital life force in living things. Your psyche is that part of you which is unique to you. It is your individual character or personality.

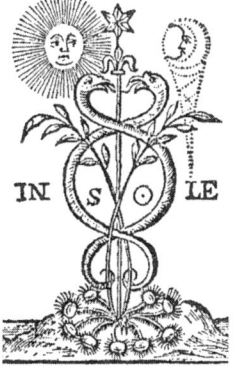

Spirit illuminates and guides the soul, while soul receives impressions from spirit above and body below. Spirit is fixed, while soul is mutable. Together they form a bridge between the divine and material realms. Spirit works through soul to affect matter, while soul can be refined through spiritual practices to become more receptive to spirit.

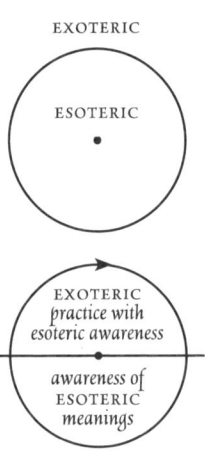

UPPER: Circle as boundary.
LOWER: Circle as orbit.

ABOVE: Hermes instructing a student in the secret Hermetic arts. The tree of nature is adorned with the exoteric sun and moon and five planets. Illustrated in circles all around are seven esoteric meanings of these seven heavenly bodies, which are related to their qualities.

ABOVE: Etruscan wall painting from Tomba degli Auguri [c. 530 BC] showing two augurs reading the language of the birds, divining meaning from the symbols of nature around them.

Quality & Sympathy
esoteric and exoteric, invisible and visible

Hermeticism, like Platonism, proposes that within every thing there is a *quality*—its essential characteristic or 'virtue', its true nature or purpose in the cosmic order. Take a coffee mug. It has its own specific *quantity* of material, colour, and shape, but behind these is always the unchanging quality or idea of "container" or "vessel".

In Hermeticism, things with similar qualities have sympathetic affinities, creating vast networks of correspondences and influences. For example, plants with sharp spikes share qualities with spears, and therefore the warlike planet Mars. This reading of symbol and the quality that stands behind appearances was central to the art of divination, known in Europe of the Middle Ages as 'the language of the birds' (*lower opposite*).

The inner qualities of things are generally revealed by their outer appearance or form, but things also have *occult* (hidden) qualities which can only be discovered through careful study and experience. Finally, all qualities are understood as either being *active*, producing effects on other things, and/or *passive*, receiving influences from other things.

This traditional way of seeing things is reflected in the terms EXOTERIC (the appearance) and ESOTERIC (the invisible cause, what stands behind, what is immanent). Humans have a technical exoteric side, begun in the crafts and formalised in the sciences, and a symbolic esoteric side, that sees the qualities of things, poetry, dreams and visions. Like the two sides of our brains they often work together. A good example is music, which is technically demanding but results in something purely qualitative.

ABOVE: *The aspirant peers through the ordinary appearance of the everyday world, to glimpse the hidden order and causality that lies behind it. This is the fundamental impetus that has led to so many of the great developments in the arts and sciences of humanity. Flammarion, 1888.*

LEFT: *The search for ultimate reality is the central focus of spiritual traditions worldwide. The Arthurian mythos, which became entwined with Hermetic ideas in the Middle Ages, often had heroes encountering a strange creature known as the* QUESTING BEAST, *an initial catalyst of inspired curiosity that prompts us to endure trials and perils in the search for understanding.*

GNOSIS
attention, thinking, and imagination

"What do you want to hear and see; what do you want to learn and know from your understanding?"—these are the first spoken words of the Hermetic corpus, uttered by Poimandres, the Universal Mind, to Hermes. They point to the central purpose of the Hermetic pursuit: *understanding* and the pursuit of knowledge. This is not the everyday type of knowledge about data, facts or current events, but a deeper knowing of the hidden natures of things, the knowledge of what it is to be conscious—*gnosis*. Prerequisite to this is *prosochē*, the faculty of focused attention, a continuous awareness of the present moment undisturbed by thought, emotion, or sensation, with constant awareness of divine presence.

Gnosis involves an inner realisation, an immediate apprehension of truth, a union with what is known. It transcends the duality of subject-object division and is thus transformative rather than merely informative. Gnosis is achieved in progressive stages via the careful study of Hermetic principles, meditation, contemplation of symbols, and the experience of practical operations.

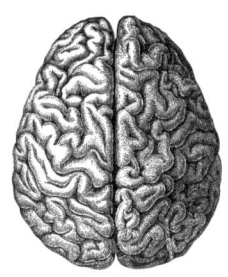

Our bilateral brains work as a synchronized pair. The left side deals with language, logic, sequential analysis and detail; the right side with spaces, patterns, music, context, creativity and overview. The Hermetic pursuit similarly straddles boundaries, portals, and liminal thresholds, connecting the known and unknown, science and magic, theology and craft, reality and illusion.

UPPER: The perfected soul as a woman or anima, in an image of perfect harmony. The solar and lunar forces, the five planets are perfectly balanced. The whole of nature and the elements are in accord. "Do you see, O son, how many bodies we have to pass through, how many bands of daimons, through how many series of repetitions and cycles of the stars, before we hasten to the One alone?"
Corpus Hermeticum IV

LOWER: "Let Nature be your guide, and let your art follow her closely; you will err if she is not your companion on the way. Let reason be your staff. Experience will brighten the lights to help discern what lies far ahead. Let reading be a lamp to illuminate the darkness, so you may prudently navigate the myriad things and words".
From Atalanta Fugiens by Michael Maier, Frankfurt 1618.

FACING PAGE: The seven governors and the androgynous human are formed in the cosmic egg within the formless primordial substance of the Materia Prima, which is everywhere and nowhere.

LIBERATION OF THE SOUL
restoring the lost harmony

According to the *Poimandres*, the union of material Nature with the Human's light of *Nous* and *Logos*, lit by the life of soul, produces the *"most wondrous of wonders"*, the birth of seven androgynous humans. After a cycle of revolutions, God splits these into male and female, telling them to *"multiply and keep multiplying"*—reminding them that only those with *Nous* will recognise their own immortality.

Here dwells the peril, for now clothed in a mortal body with free will, humans are subject to their passions. According to the web of fate, destructive forces called *daimons* are now drawn in, tangling and obscuring the light within: greed, wrath, insatiability, cruelty, lust for wealth, craving for glory and honours, the urge to dominate others—a list as long as human error. These passions are ruled by the seven governors, and their positions at the moment of each human birth—a map of the individual psyche studied by natal astrology (*see p.32*).

MATERIA PRIMA.

To mitigate this, Hermetic practices of 'soul medicine', especially prayer and meditation, focus attention on the present cosmic moment to restore balance, countering the passions with virtues, polishing the soul like a mirror to reflect the light of *Nous* and awaken the eye of the heart.

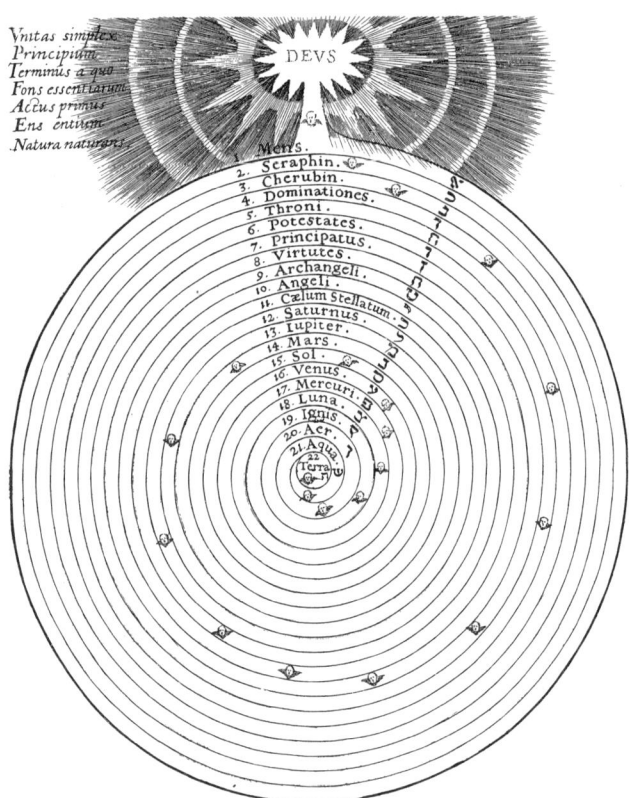

ABOVE: A Renaissance imagining of the Hermetic Cosmos, Robert Fludd, 1619. God (Deus), at the top with entities and essences to the left, gives rise to the outer sphere of Mens, Divine Mind, followed by three hierarchies of three Angelic Orders (these nine spheres only emerge in the 5th/6th centuries), then the sphere of the fixed stars, the seven spheres of governance (the planets), and finally the four elements, with Earth at the centre.
FACING PAGE: LEFT: The Luminous Logos inseminating moist, dark Nature. RIGHT: The four philosophical elements and their symbols: (left to right) Earth, Water, Air and Fire.

CREATION
a love story

In the Hermetic tradition, the cosmos is created by eternity. Book 11 of the *Corpus Hermeticum* states that "*God makes eternity; eternity makes the cosmos; the cosmos makes time; time makes becoming*".

The moist darkness of nature, inseminated by the luminous *Logos*, uses "*her own elements and her offspring the souls*" to make a *phenomenal* image of the *noumenon*, the light world of *Nous*. The *Nous* then sends a restatement of itself, a "*god of fire and spirit*", that assumes the role of *Demiurge* or cosmic architect and fashions seven governors (*the planets, opposite*). This draws the *Logos* upwards, *Logos* and *Demiurge* fusing together, and begins the endless motion of the seven spheres. Their rule is known as *heimarmene*, the cosmic web of fate, which like the *Ouroboros* serpent, forever devours itself (*see page 58*).

From the androgynous *Nous* a beautiful human is born, greatly beloved by all, who then moves down through the spheres and approaches Nature. She sees his image reflected in her waters, while he sees her shape is like his own, image sings to image, and they embrace.

"I am the light you saw, the Nous, your God, who existed before the watery nature that appeared out of darkness. The luminous Logos who comes from Nous"

"Know this: that in you which sees and hears is the Logos, and your Nous is God, they are not separate for their union is life" POIMANDRES

ABOVE: The Eternal Light. The etymology of the name 'Poimandres' still puzzles scholars. 'Shepherd of man' approximates in ancient Greek. Roots in the Egyptian language, deriving Poimandres from terms meaning 'the knowledge of Rē' have also been suggested.

FACING PAGE: Falcon headed Re, or Ra, was the Egyptian solar principle of order.

Logos & Nous
a vision of language and light

The first event in the first book of the *Corpus Hermeticum* is Hermes Trismegistus' vision of the Cosmic Consciousness, named *Poimandres*. While in a sleep-like state, contemplating *"the things that truly are"*, Hermes is confronted by an infinitely large presence, a living being of light, named *"Poimandres, the Nous of Power"* (or *"Nous of Authority"*). *Nous* is a subtle word with no direct cognate, variously translated as mind, God, intellect, consciousness, or understanding. It is an illumination. Hermes is told to hold his questions in his *Nous*, his own light mind, which then proceeds to show him visions within the vision.

Poimandres becomes a *"clear and joyful light"*, and then darkness coils about him like a snake, transforming into a watery substance that gives off smoke and roars mournfully. Hermes hears a cry *"like a voice of light"*, and the *Nous* sends down a flame, *"a holy LOGOS ... nimble and piercing and active at the same time"*, which separates air and fire ('above') from earth and water ('below').

Logos is the Living Creative Verb, language, speech, discourse, and reason. The scholar Wouter Hanegraaff describes *Logos* as *"the specific capacity of immediate vision and audition inherent in the Nous"*. As Poimandres says, *"they are not separate for their union is life"*. Thus his own *Nous*-and-*Logos* sees the divine *Nous*-and-*Logos*, and observer and observed are one and the same. *Nous* witnessing *Nous*.

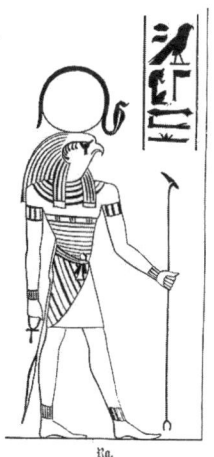

Ra.

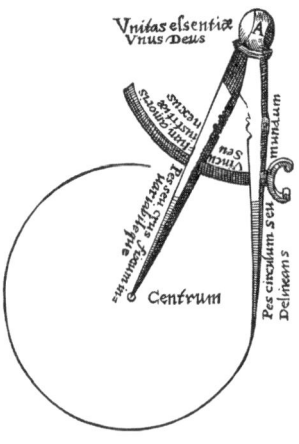

LEFT: The Divine Compass by Robert Fludd, with the unity of essence of the One God on its headpiece, decorated with an 'A', presumably meaning Alpha, the first letter. The other parts of the compass are given a Demiurgic quality: God as Geometer; "the fixed and unchanging foot or leg"; "the circular or world-drawing foot"; the adjustment bar is "the bond of love, or union of justice". The Compass is the only hand tool that is not a model of itself, the planes of the ruler and blade are themselves planes, only the compass holds the radius in waiting for the circle. From Utriusque cosmi historia T. II, 1619.

LEFT: Rosa Celeste: Dante and Beatrice gaze upon the highest Heaven, The Empyrean. Canto 31, The Paradiso, Divine Comedy, Dante Alighieri 1321. Gustav Doré, 1892. FACING PAGE: God as the vanishing point of a perspective grid. 'Ab Uno' means 'From One'.

God is: "everything and there is nothing outside God, even that which does not exist." - The Definitions (p.3); "the first form, prior to the beginning of the beginningless and endless." - Poimandres. "Invisible … Unbegotten, Self-Begotten, and Begotten." - Discourse on the Ogdoad and the Ennead.

THE UNIQUE
dancing around the centre

The Hermetic texts resort to puzzles and paradoxes when speaking of—or declining to speak of—God. To speak of what cannot be spoken of they use contradictions like the '*God beyond God*', or the '*God prior to God*' (the *Ain Sof* of the Kabbalah), which are designed to stimulate reflective thought in the immortal part of the soul capable of understanding eternal truths, the *Nous*. Hermeticists hold that this Source, Unity, the One, the wonderful Idea of Ideas, can only be known through the duality of language and thought. Only by opening our *noetic* senses can the *Nous* in us know itself through us.

The Hermetic saying "*God is an infinite sphere whose centre is everywhere and whose circumference is nowhere*" appears in the 12th-century French *Book of the 24 Philosophers* as one of 24 answers to the question "What is God?". The Hermetic view is of God both transcendent and immanent—both utterly beyond and utterly here. God is the Cosmos, and God created the Cosmos, "*all is one, all is from the One*". God is the All, existing everywhere, including within us. Not just the infinite circle, but also the point within the circle, Good, Beautiful and True. In the words of the American poet Robert Frost [1874-1963]:

We dance round in a ring and suppose,
But the Secret sits in the middle and knows.

change on all levels. By breaking down existing forms, separating their elements, refining them, and then recombining them into new forms, matter can be perfected and the soul purified. Everything contains a spark of the divine, and everything seeks to return to the source.

5. **Knowledge** (*Gnosis*). Humans can attain direct experiential knowledge of divine reality. Theoretical understanding and practical operations can lead to direct insight, personal transformation and transcendence of duality. A unity of knower, knowing, and known.

6. **Human Potential**. Humans occupy a unique position in the Cosmos. As simultaneously material, rational, and spiritual beings who can operate on multiple levels, humans have the potential for personal transformation and perfection, bridging the worlds above and below, and transforming the material world too.

7. **Nature as Living Reality**. Nature is a living expression of divine mind. The universe is a living, conscious being. All things are alive, conscious, and intelligent—minerals, plants, animals, planets, stars. We should learn nature's language, and work with her.

8. **Unity of All Things**. Everything that emerges from source is connected and affects everything else. Apparent separation is an illusion. All forces, polarities, and principles balance in opposition. Unity extends through all levels of reality: spiritual (shared consciousness), vital (shared life force), and material (shared elements).

The Tenets of Hermeticism
the eightfold path

Hermeticism is the syncretic fusion of ancient Egyptian traditions with Greek and other Near Eastern philosophies, poorly preserved in scattered fragments, and famously difficult to define. However, a few core themes can be outlined:

1. **Divine Unity and Emanation.** There is one unified supreme divine principle, transcendent and immanent, beyond all qualities or descriptions. All reality emanates from it in descending levels of manifestation, from subtle to dense, from spiritual to material, to the Divine Mind (*Nous*), to the Universal World Soul, to Nature, and to the physical universe.

2. **Correspondence.** The microcosm reflects the macrocosm ('*As above, so below*'). Thus human nature reflects divine nature, spiritual principles manifest in physical forms, and inner states match external reality. Each level of reality corresponds to others, and understanding one level will give insight into others.

3. **Mediation and Intermediaries.** The universe is hierarchical with multiple levels. There are intelligences, beings and forces that mediate between these levels, from planets, angels and daimons to sacred numbers and names. With proper timing, channels and procedures, humans can act as mediators between the realms, channelling higher influences downward and raising lower substances upward.

4. **Transformation and Transmutation.** What happens in one sphere affects others, so we can do practical and spiritual work, effecting

Tis true without lying, certain and most true.
That which is Below is like that which is Above, and that which is Above is like that which is Below, to do the miracle of One only thing. And as all things have been and arose from One by the mediation of One: so all things have their birth from this One thing by adaptation. The Sun is its father, the Moon its mother, the Wind hath carried it in its belly, the Earth is its nurse. The father of all perfection in the whole World is here. Its force or power is entire if it be converted into Earth. Separate thou the earth from the fire, the subtle from the gross sweetly with great industry. It ascends from the Earth to the Heaven and again it descends to the Earth and receives the force of things Superior and inferior. By this means you shall have the glory of the whole World and thereby all obscurity shall fly from you. Its Force is above all force, for it vanquishes every subtle thing and penetrates every solid thing. So was the World created. From this are and do come admirable adaptations whereof the means is here in this. Hence I am called Hermes Trismegist, having the three parts of the Philosophy of the whole World. That which I have said of the operation of the Sun is accomplished and ended.

ABOVE: The very short but hugely influential text of the Emerald Tablet, supposedly discovered by Balinas in the 8th century, translated here by Isaac Newton around 1680.
LEFT: Heinrich Khunrath's 17th century image of the Emerald Tablet as a mountain.

THE EMERALD TABLET
mirror mirror

The philosopher Jiddu Krishnamurti [1895–1986] once said *"You are the world and the world is you"*, perfectly mirroring the famous lines of the *Tabula Smaragdina*, the *Emerald Tablet* of Hermes Trismegistus. Likely first written in Arabic, the earliest extant copy appears in an Arabic book attributed to the 8th-century figure Balinas (or Pseudo-Apollonius of Tyana), who claimed he found the tablet in the city of Tyana, in modern Turkey, buried under a statue of Hermes in a tomb holding a golden-throned corpse clutching a tablet of emerald.

The Tablet says what is hinted at in the Poimandres dialogue (*see p.18*), that humans beings are a microcosmos, corresponding to and living within, above or alongside a macrocosmos: *"As above so below"*. It says that everything comes from one substance, and instructs us to separate the subtle from the gross, *"sweetly with great industry"*.

LEFT: The Seven Liberal Arts, shown here as branches of the Tree of Knowledge which emanates from Philosophy. The three liberal arts which deal with language are known as the Trivium of Grammar, Logic and Rhetoric. The four Liberal Arts which deal with number are known as the Quadrivium of Arithmetic, Geometry, Music and Astronomy. Woodcut frontispiece from Margarita Philosophica, by Gregor Reisch, 1503.

The heavens, a perceptible god, administer all bodies whose growth and decline have been charged to the sun and moon. But god, who is their maker, is himself governor of heaven and of soul itself and of all things that are in the world. From all these, all governed by the same god, a continuous influence carries through the world and through the soul of all kinds and all forms throughout nature. God prepared matter as a receptacle for omniform forms, but nature, imaging matter with forms by means of the four elements, causes all things to reach as far as heaven so that they will be pleasing in the sight of god. ASCLEPIVS 3

THE ASCLEPIUS DIALOGUE
and the Ogtoad and Ennead

From about the fifth century until the fifteenth, the only substantial ancient Hermetic text known in western Europe was the dialogue known as *Asclepius*, translated from a mostly-lost Greek original known as the *Perfect Discourse*. It takes the form of a short dialogue between divine Hermes and three of his students, including Asclepius, who receive spiritual and philosophical teachings. All the fundamental ideas of Hermeticism are covered: the seven spheres of the cosmos, the creation and role of nature and man, and the correct forms of philosophy (there is also much mention of the last days of Egypt and how the temples of Kem will fall into ruin).

The dialogue discusses the Quadrivium, the four liberal arts which deal with number (*see opposite top*), saying that these should be employed to study and wonder at the majesty of creation rather than to confuse and obscure true philosophy. These subjects were to deeply influence medieval arts and architecture many centuries later (*see page 36*), and eventually form the basis for the modern sciences (*see page 54*).

Another Hermetic document, found in 1945 at Nag Hammadi in Upper Egypt, gives more detail. Known as *Discourse on the Eighth and the Ninth*, it describes the three realms of the divine world that exist outside of the seven planetary governors and the web of fate. The eighth sphere is the realm of the fixed stars and perfected souls (humans who have found *gnosis*, as well as beings created of pure soul by the *Nous*). The ninth sphere is the unbounded world of Mind/*Nous*, forms and archetypes. The tenth sphere is ultimate unity, the source, God, the One that cannot be described.

LEFT: Image of Hermes from the mosaic floor of Sienna cathedral, Italy. The Latin text at the bottom of the image, translates to "Hermes Mercurius Trismegistus, contemporary of Moses."

BELOW & OPPOSITE: Hermes Trismegistus shown holding an armillary sphere aloft, symbol of the heavens, and pointing to the Earth below. As patron of alchemy, magic, the arts, philosophy, initiation and psychopomp, he balances the polarities of being.

HERMES TRISMEGISTUS
the thrice great

Perhaps in Alexandria, in the first century CE, among the scholars at the great Library, Hermes/Thoth began to be called Hermes Trismegistus. "Thrice greatest" was an appellation given to Thoth that translates into Greek as *trismegistos*. "Thrice great" (a less illogically-inflated honour) is widely used today. Perhaps he was named thus because he was the father of three arts: alchemy, astrology, and magic. Or perhaps he had truly approached the holy of holies, purified, annointed, and crowned, like the alchemist's stone. No one knows.

Some thought of him as a god. Others as human. Some as both. Some thought of him as a contemporary or teacher of Moses, perhaps even Moses himself. Others said he was a student of Thoth. He was usually portrayed as human, an older man, holding a book or an armillary sphere (*opposite and below*).

As the embodiment of wisdom, Hermes' name was affixed to dozens of remarkable texts combining Egyptian, Greek, and other ideas, dealing with subjects ranging from the occult sciences of the Technical Hermetica to the particular brand of pious philosophical worship discussed in the theoretical or spiritual tomes. The ancient Hermetica which survive today (*see p.3*) are likely the meagre remnant of what would have been a flourishing literature.

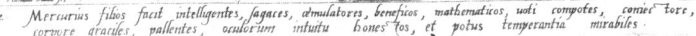

Mercurius filios facit intelligentes, sagaces, aemulatores, beneficos, mathematicos, uoti compotes, comes tore, corpore graciles, pallentes, oculorum intuitu honestos, et potus temperantia mirabiles.

ABOVE: Mercury, with his winged feet, rides in his chariot across the sky. The signs of Virgo and Gemini indicate which people belong to his sphere of influence: learned scientists, astrologers, musicians, artists, sculptors, merchants, and doctors. Johannes Galle, Antwerp, 1638. LEFT: Mercury as Herm, boundary marker and guide. FACING PAGE: Hermes invents the very first lyre from a tortoise shell, and gifts it to Apollo, who gives Hermes his famous caduceus in return.

MERCURIAL HERMES
messenger of the gods

The Greek god Hermes, son of Zeus and the nymph Maia, was a precocious child. The *Homeric Hymn to Hermes* describes the first three days of his life, when he turns a tortoise into the first lyre, invents fire-starting and steals Apollo's golden cattle (driving them backward while also wearing his shoes backward to obscure the direction). When called to task for the theft, Hermes so impresses the gods that he is himself raised to godhood, gifting his lyre to Apollo and in return being gifted the famous caduceus (*below*) and the *mantic* or divinatory arts.

The name Hermes is linked to the *hermai*—ancient stone cairns and monoliths used as wayguides, later carved with heads and phalluses, indicating Hermes' creative potential, and dominion over boundaries. As a psychopomp (a guide of souls), Hermes moves between realms and can pass messages between the gods, the underworld, and the earth.

Hermes' Roman counterpart is Mercury, fast, fluid and as hard to pin down as quicksilver. Like Hermes he wears *talaria* or winged sandals of imperishable gold, forged by Hephaestus/Vulcan, imparting the darting speed of a bird, and a winged helmet, or a wide brimmed hat known as a *petasos*. Mercury gives us the words *merchant* and *merchandise*, as well as the *mercurial* humour of the trickster. He is patron to communicators, artists, orators, traders, conmen, and thieves.

ABOVE LEFT: Thoth or Djehuti, bringer of the arts and sciences, inventor of writing, god of the moon, measure, magic and the underworld. ABOVE RIGHT: Thoout, Thoth Deux fois Grand, le Second Hermès, from Panthéon Égyptien, Champollion, 1823. FACING PAGE: The Sacred Ibis on the bank of the Nile. LEFT: Thoth as baboon, with a lunar crown. Instead of the word GOD, the Ancient Egyptians described their pantheon using the word NETER, meaning quality, principle or nature (which sounds like our word 'nature' but no etymological connection exists). Specific animals were selected to represent particular qualities of different Neters, e.g. the remarkable digestive qualities of the jackal, able to break everything down equally, makes it the perfect image for Anubis, judge of judges.

THOTH
bringer of culture, science and magic

When the Greeks encountered Egyptian religion, they identified the Egyptian god Thoth with their god Hermes, creating the composite figure Hermes Trismegistus. Thoth, the 'dual inward being', had inventing writing, and from 600 BC was also the god of wisdom, the Moon, and the arts and sciences. He was also surveyor of the cosmos, the gods' scribe, and later their judge. He was a courier and a trickster with magic charms, often using his intellect to trick enemies or prospective lovers. The Ancient Egyptians called him *Djehuty* or *Tehuti* (becoming *Thoth* in Greek, and *Thōout* or *Thout* in Coptic). Given his instigation of so many human practices, perhaps *Thought* would be an appropriate name for him, for *Djehuty* is discernment, judgment, measure, and learning.

The qualities of the animals that make up the forms of the ancient Egyptian gods (or *neters*, 'principles') reveal many things about their nature or qualities. The image of Thoth with the head of an ibis (a lunar night bird known to catch snakes, that digs around in the dirt with its long curved beak on the shore where land meets water) reveals qualities of precision, and the love of thresholds and hidden things.

TECHNICAL HERMETICA

GREEK:

The Wandering of the Influences
The Nechepsos-Petosiris texts
The Art of Eudoxus
Liber Hermetis
The Brontologion (thunderstorms)
The Peri seismōn (earthquakes)
The Book of Asclepius (Myriogenesis)
Holy Book of Hermes to Asclepius
The Fifteen Stars, Stones, Plants and Images
The Cyranides

ARABIC:

The Book of Hermes on the Revolutions of the Years of the Nativities
Carmen Astrologicum
The Book of the Secrets of the Stars
The Book of the Exposition of the Key to the Stars
The Secret of Creation and the Art of Nature or The Book of Causes
The Emerald Tablet
The Epistle of the Secret
The Commentary on the Book of the Wise Hermes on the Properties of Snakes and Scorpions
The Circle of Letters of the Alphabet
The Book of Hermes on Alchemy

SPIRITUAL HERMETICA

THE CORPUS HERMETICUM:

I - Poimandres
II - Theory of Movement, Space and Emptiness
III - A Sacred Discourse of Hermes
IV - Salvation through Nous
V - Theology of God
VI - God, the Good and the Passions
VII - Hermetic Sermon
VIII - Theory of God and the Cosmos
IX - Theory of Perception
X - The Key
XI - The Hermetic Definitions
XII - Nous, Logos and God
XIII - Creation and God
XIV - The Letter of Hermes to Asclepius
XV - To Asclepius: Discourse on the Sun
XVI - God as Ultimate Source
XVII - Incorporeal reflected in corporeal
XVIII - Praise of God

The Discourse on the Eighth and Ninth (from the Nag Hammadi Library)
The Stobean Hermetic Fragments
The Asclepius dialogue - The Perfect Discourse

ABOVE: Classical texts of the theoretical Hermetica surviving mostly in Greek. LEFT: a selection of Technical Hermetica from antiquity, many of which survive only as titles or scattered quotations in later authors.

The Hermetic Labyrinth
Egyptian theology through a Grecian lens

Egypt was conquered by Alexander the Great around 330 BC. Ruled from the cosmopolitan capital city of Alexandria, home to half a million Egyptians, Greeks, Jews, and others, Hellenistic Egypt was the home of the first Hermetists. 'Hermetica' are Greek works attributed to the sage Hermes and sometimes to a supporting cast of characters including his disciples Tat, Asclepios, and other. The earliest are the 'technical Hermetica', dealing with the natural sciences, alchemy, astrology, magic, and the manipulation of natural forces.

Later, probably in the period of Roman rule (from 31 BC), another type of Hermetic text emerges, known as 'philosophic', 'spiritual', or 'theoretical Hermetica', dealing with philosophy, divine knowledge, and the soul's salvation through assimilation to the divine Mind. The most important collection of theoretical Hermetica is the Byzantine Greek compilation known as the *Corpus Hermeticum*; to it is often added the stand-alone Latin Hermetic dialogue known as *Asclepius*, translated from a lost Greek original.

Other theoretical Hermetica from antiquity survive in Greek in the collection of the fifth-century writer John of Stobi, a.k.a Stobæus. Many Hermetica, both technical and spiritual, survive from late antiquity only in translations (Latin, Coptic, Armenian, Arabic, and more), a range showing the wide influence of these texts.

Further Græco-Egyptian Hermetic works include those of the Platonist philosopher Iamblichus of Chalcis [245-325 BC], the fourth-century alchemist Zosimos of Panopolis, and others. Attempts to frame Hermetic ideas as a direct chain of transmission remain inconclusive.

Introduction

Hermeticism is not a religion or a consistent philosophy, nor is it a science, an art, an ideology or a dogma. It is not magic or alchemy, astrology or medicine, law or poetry. Rather, it is a mode of perception, a core state of consciousness that makes these arts possible. It is said to be the teachings of the visionary teacher Hermes Trismegistus, whose history is but rumour and anecdote and who remains as mysterious as his mythological antecedents, Thoth, Hermes, and Mercury.

Hermeticism emerges from Græco-Egyptian culture as ancient Egypt draws her last breath, over two millennia ago. Valentie Tomberg calls it *"the communal soul of religion, science and art"*. For two thousand years, it has been one of the most persistent strains of thought in European, Middle Eastern and North African culture.

The texts that make up the specific set of spiritual teachings known as the *Corpus Hermeticum* (along with the magical, astrological, and medical manuals of the Technical Hermetica) have passed for centuries through the selection bias of translators, editors, and improvers, yet they remain fruitful and vital. Great thinkers, mystics, poets, and philosophers have long been inspired by the mysteries woven through these few and often fragmentary works. Hermeticism's influence extends to the founding of cities, secret societies, great works of art and architecture, and foundational breakthroughs in chemistry, physics, and astronomy.

The focus of Hermeticism is light, an intelligent benevolent light we ourselves are an image of. A light that connects and corresponds to all that is. A light that we can embody, if we approach with wonder, reverence and awe.

Introduction	1
The Hermetic Labyrinth	2
Thoth	4
Mercurial Hermes	6
Hermes Trismegistus	8
The Asclepius Dialogue	10
The Emerald Tablet	12
The Tenets of Hermeticism	14
The Unique	16
Logos and Nous	18
Creation	20
Liberation of the Soul	22
Gnosis	24
Quality and Sympathy	26
Pneuma and Psyche	28
Lights in the Mind	30
Secrets of the Stars	32
Magic and Medicine	34
Hermetic Religions	36
The Renaissance	38
Mediation	40
The Alchemist's Art	42
Solve et Coagula	44
The Cross & the Rose	46
Secret Orders	48
The Age of Laws	50
The Perennial Tradition	52
Everything is Connected	54
The Conscious Universe	56

Thanks to my editors: Adam Tetlow, John Martineau, Earl Fontainelle.

Illustration from page 23 of 'Lumen de Lumine, or, A New Magical Light Discovered and Communicated to the World', by Eugenius Philalethes (real name Thomas Vaughan), 1651.

HERMETICISM
THE SECRET TRADITION

Kenneth W. Davis